THE GREATEST
Golfing Tips
IN THE WORLD ®

by

John Cook

Illustrated by Graham Robson

Public Eye Publications

A Public Eye Publications Book

www.thegreatestintheworld.com

Illustrations:
Graham Robson, 'Drawing the Line'
info@dtline.co.uk

Cover design:
Setsquare Creative Design Consultants

Cover photo:
Clive Nichols
www.clivenichols.com

Layout design:
Bloomfield Ltd.

Copy editor:
Bronwyn Robertson
www.theartsva.com

Series creator / editor:
Steve Brookes

This first edition published in 2005 by
Public Eye Publications, PO Box 3182,
Stratford-upon-Avon, Warwickshire CV37 7XW

Text and Illustrations Copyright © 2005 - Public Eye Publications

'The Greatest In The World' Copyright © 2004 - Anne Brookes

A CIP catalogue record for this book is available from the British Library
ISBN 1-905151-05-5

Printed and bound by Ashford Colour Press Limited, Gosport, Hampshire PO13 0FW

I would like to dedicate this book to:-

My Dad – Philip
My Mum – Sylvia

My Wife – Karen
My Sons – Mat & Ben

They truly are a great family

A big thank you!

Gary Player and Family

Apart from my immediate family, Gary and his family have been the biggest influence in my professional golfing career. Gary, you treated me like a brother, I hasten to add, much younger brother! Your help and guidance, the hours and hours we spent working on our golf swings has helped me to become hopefully one of the best golf teachers in the world. I do not believe I ever go through a day of coaching without bringing your name up.
Thank you for being my friend.

Butch, Dick, Bill and Craig Harmon

Without doubt, the best golfing family in the world!
Their father, Claude, won the Masters in 1948 and a great deal of the golfing knowledge and experience they have, comes straight from him.
I have only known you all for a few years but the time we have spent together, coaching the juniors from Great Britain and Ireland has been tremendous fun.
You are the greatest golf teachers in the world, it is an honour to know you.

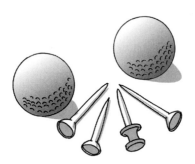

Contents

A few words from Gary Player...

I have known John for over 30 years. I consider him to be a close friend and a wonderful teacher of the game of golf - certainly one of the very finest short game coaches teaching players today.

Our friendship and the adventures we shared during the long hot summers that John stayed with me on my farm in South Africa, when I was the number one golfer in the world and he was a fresh faced young pro bursting with confidence on the back of winning the English Amateur Championship and British Youths Championship, can be seen as an example of the good things and opportunities that this game can give us. I have been lucky enough to travel the world many times over and to meet people from all walks of life through golf. In an age when ethics and values are constantly undermined, this sport truly brings out the best in people by encompassing the virtues of honour, respect, hard work and personal achievement - all of which matter more than ever in today's modern world!

John and I share many of the same ideas in playing the game. He possesses a wonderful intuitive gift for imparting his knowledge and technical instruction both simply and effectively. He is a teacher with both humour and empathy and a man who is respected throughout the golfing community. The tips and advice in this book will help your golf game immensely and I hope will bring you many hours of fun on the course. You can use the book time and time again for reference and I hope you have as much enjoyment reading these amusing and informative pearls of wisdom on the game as I have.

Gary Player

The Greatest Golfing Tips In The World

Gain match play advantage

You can get off to a great start in match play by asserting yourself on the first tee. As soon as you meet your opponent on the tee, tell him the number of ball you are using; if he was going to use the same number he'll be forced to change his ball. This may be your opponent's lucky number ball which he has to change because you asserted yourself!

Simplify the hardest shot in the game

It is widely recognized that the 50 to 60 yard bunker shot is the hardest in the game. The problem is that we are caught between it being a splash shot and long bunker shot where we catch the ball clean. Normally we swing far too hard at the ball, having convinced ourselves that it is a splash shot, a message is sent to our brain during the downswing that says we are swinging too hard at the shot, so in a split second we take too much sand and the ball only goes half-way. If the ball was lying in the grass outside the bunker it would be an easy shot, wouldn't it? You would just pitch the ball onto the green.

Next time you are faced with the 50 to 60 yard bunker shot, play it the same as you would play it from the grass, use a sand wedge, hit the ball, then the sand and only hit as hard as you would from the grass. The little message will not be sent to your brain saying you are swinging too hard and the result will surprise you.

Take the flag out for short chips

Next time you are practising your chipping from just off the side of the green try leaving the pin in for a couple of shots, then play the same shots with the pin out. You will find that when the pin is out you will be more inclined to try to hole the shot than you would if you leave the pin in. This is totally psychological, but it works!

The ball will go with the slope

One of the most common questions I am asked when playing a course with lots of sloping lies is 'Which way will the ball go off a particular slope?'. When you are addressing the ball that is above your feet, the ball will fly a little left of where you are aiming. When the ball is below your feet, the ball will fly a little right of where you are aiming. An easy way to remember is that the ball will always go in the direction of the slope.

The shot under pressure

Let's imagine for a minute that you are on the last hole and you need a par to win - drive the ball on the fairway and hit the second shot onto the green, two putts and you're there.

Then reality comes in - a crooked drive, a chip out of the woods, miss the green with your approach and so on. The way the Tour Professionals cope is by trying to make the smoothest, most balanced swing they have ever made. This is a great tip for those of you who get into a winning position but do not manage to pull off the win enough times.

On the green, pace is more important than line

If a caddy ever points to a line before he has asked you how you see the ball going into the hole, do not ask him for his advice again. The first and most important thing to decide when you are reading the green is how you see the ball going into the hole. Do you see it dying into the hole or hitting the back of the hole and dropping in; the line will be totally different for both. Having decided on the pace, then decide on the line.

Perfect your strike - on the beach!

Not many of us are fortunate enough to live near a beach and even fewer of us live near to a beach on which you can hit a golf ball. If you are one of these lucky people or you happen to be going on holiday to such a place then take advantage of the opportunity. The sand must be damp and flat and, for obvious safety reasons, you have to be well away from other people. Practise with your irons, sand wedge to long iron, and don't be happy until you can hit the ball first, then the sand. In no time at all your entire ball striking will improve.

Don't be too ambitious from the rough

There is a phrase used that I believe is worth listening to: "Take your medicine". This means that when you have driven the ball into a bad place; do not try the shot that may only come off one in ten times. Accept the fact that you have finished in a bad position and get the ball back in play.

Hole out before going to the tee

Confidence plays a massive part in golf; sometimes you just cannot see the ball going into the hole. Next time you play, just before you go to the first tee, go onto the putting green and putt 10 balls into the hole from 18 inches. You will get used to seeing the ball drop in and this will give you all the confidence you need.

Great shots into the wind

For some reason our natural instinct tells us to hit the ball much harder into the wind, I suppose it is because we still want the ball to travel maximum distance, even though the wind is blowing into our faces. The problems start when we lose our balance by trying to hit the ball too hard. Also the extra club head speed that is created gives the ball much more backspin which elevates the ball almost into orbit and of course the ball is blown off line. Try doing the opposite; hit the ball soft into the wind. You will maintain your balance and the ball will fly on a much more penetrating trajectory. Hit the ball as hard as you like downwind.

Arrive in plenty of time

It is very important to find out what is a suitable amount of time for you to allow for travelling from the airport or your hotel to the golf course. Some people like to arrive at the course an hour before teeing off. This gives about $1/2$ hour to hit the ball and $1/4$ hour to get in some putting. Other players like to arrive only $3/4$ hour before the start of their game. Many amateurs I have seen tend to arrive with so little time to spare that they end up tying their shoe laces on the way to the first tee! Then they wonder why they get off to a bad start!

Tips on reading the greens

No matter how good your putting stroke, if you hit the ball on the wrong line, the ball will not go into the hole. Reading the green is obviously a very important part of putting, so take your time and notice more things about the green.

The very first thing you must do is to decide how fast you would like the ball to go into the hole, do you see it dying in or do you see it hitting the back of the hole? Having made that decision, you can start to look for slopes and grain or nap. This is the direction the grass is growing; if you see that the grass looks dark, the grain is coming towards you, slowing down the putt, if the green gives the appearance of being light in colour or shiny, the grain or nap is going away from you, speeding up the putt.

The slope can be seen from behind the ball most of the time but if you cannot see the slope from there, stand behind the hole and look back towards the ball. On all long putts, look from the side to help you decide whether the putt is uphill or downhill. Having picked a line, commit to it!

Putt to a tee

Stick a tee into the practice putting green and practise putting to it. You are setting your sights higher by trying to hit the tee with the ball. When you go onto the course the hole looks the size of a bucket. You can do this on the carpet at home by turning the tee up side down.

Keep the grip light

One of the most common faults is gripping the club too tightly, especially the driver. Whenever we try to hit the ball hard, we grip hard, so hard that the knuckles go white! In actual fact, a tight grip stops you from being able to release the club head properly through impact, eliminating much of the club head speed. Grip the club as lightly as you would hold a bird, you will have more feel, less tension and more club head speed.

Rehearse your first shot

Always warm up on the range before setting off on your round. Start with a lofted club, then hit some mid irons, followed by a few wood shots. You feel warmed up and ready to go. Not quite! Now rehearse your first tee shot with the club you intend using from the first tee. It is amazing how much easier it makes your real first tee shot.

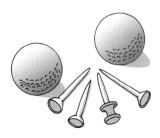

Put on your shades

Sometimes it can be very difficult to read the greens; you keep coming up with the wrong line. This is very common on sunny days so put on your sunglasses when reading the green; it makes the slope more prominent.

Look at the hole back to front

When I get to the ball on a tight driving hole and look back to the tee, it always amazes me how easy it looks. Try it next time you play. If you are able to have a practice round on the course, make a point of looking back to the tee from the middle of the fairway, this will dispel your fears about the difficulty of some of the holes.

Use the manufacturer's name

When putting, line up the manufacturer's name on your ball with the point that you are going to hit your putt towards. Make sure you have a putter that has a directional line on it and simply line it up with the manufacturer's line and strike the putt.

Tee ball high to hit it low

When you are driving into the wind, the last thing you want is for the ball to go too high. You would think that the obvious thing to do, when trying to hit the ball low with your driver, is to tee it low. When the ball is teed low it encourages a steeper approach into the ball, often resulting in too much backspin; the head wind gets under it causing the ball to fly high with no penetration.

Next time you want to hit the ball low into the wind with your driver; try teeing the ball a little higher than you would for your normal drive. Then hit the ball clean off the top of the tee, without making contact with the tee. You will find the ball flies lower with much more penetration.

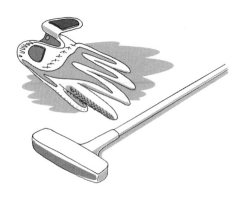

Slippery grips can be fatal

Over a period of time your grips will get dirty and slippery; it does not take long if your hands perspire. Slippery grips make you hold too tight, which stops you from releasing the club head through impact, resulting in a loss of distance. The best tip I can give you for cleaning the grips and getting them tacky is to swish the grips of each club in the dew, then let them dry naturally. The first thing to do to hit longer shots is to get those grips clean and tacky.

Check your clubs before you tee off

Any more than fourteen clubs in your bag will incur penalty shots, so before you tee off on the first hole check that you only have fourteen, and check that you have a score card, a pencil, enough balls to last the round, tees, a towel if it looks like rain, an umbrella and an energy drink. You are probably going to spend the best part of four hours on the course, so don't get caught out.

Strengths and weaknesses

Everyone will have a strong shot and a weak shot with each part of their game, yes, including Tiger Woods! There is a gap between your strong shot and your weak shot, which you need to narrow. Let me give you an example:

Tiger prefers to hit the ball with his driver with a slight fade, so a fade is his strong shot. He is not quite so confident hitting his drives with a draw, so a draw is his weak shot.

The gap between these shots for Tiger is very narrow. The gap between your favourite shaped drive and your less favourite shape may be wide. Get used to playing the golf course using your strong/favourite shaped shots and practise your weak/less favourite shaped shots on the practice ground. You will find that you will improve your weak shots and begin to play them on the course.

Don't just dry your hands

Most of us carry a towel on the side of the bag to clean the ball. It is important to carry another towel to dry your hands when they are clammy with perspiration. Make sure the towel is wet at one end and dry at the other so when your hands get clammy you can wash them then dry them. This is much better than just drying sweaty hands.

Warm up with two clubs

There have been a number of quite expensive warm up devices available to purchase over the years, but I still think that swinging with two clubs for a minute or two does the job best and is certainly cheaper.

Fun and productive short game practice

Practising short game can be boring and can therefore be a waste of time, so here is a tip that will help to make it fun and productive…

Choose four different shots to practise around the practice green, e.g. Long putt, Lob shot, Greenside bunker shot and a Chip and run shot. Check what time you start. Start with the first shot (long putt) and stay there until you hole one, then move to the next shot (lob shot) stay until you have holed it and so on until you have holed all four shots. Check the time to see how long it took you to complete. Each time you go to the practice ground carry out the same exercise and see how long it takes. If it takes an hour at first and within a week or two you can do it in ³/₄ hour, it shows a 25% improvement.

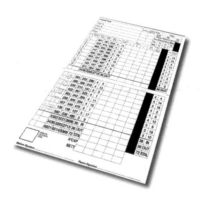

Listen - don't look!

Short putts can be a nightmare, making us frightened of them. The biggest fault I find is when a player, anxious to see if they have holed the putt, looks up too early, the shoulders open and the only way to get the ball in the hole is to steer it in. With any putt of four feet or below, putt the ball and listen for the ball to drop. This will keep your shoulders square to the line. In the interest of slow play, if you have not heard anything within ten minutes, you have missed it!!

It can still drop in!

The putt that finishes hanging over the hole is so
frustrating. The fraction of an inch putt counts as much as
a full drive from the tee. Next time this happens to you try
putting your shadow over the ball, sometimes the coolness
of the shadow causes the grass to lie flat, making the
ball topple in. Do not, however, use any other method of
helping the ball into the hole!

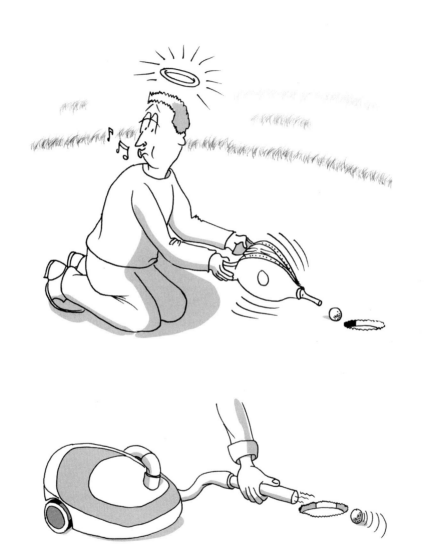

The sand wedge-putter

The mowers these days do such a wonderful job of cutting the greens and the fringes to the greens, they quite often leave sharp edges. If your ball finishes up against one of these edges, it does not leave a straightforward shot. The most difficult one is when the ball comes against the edge between the fringe grass, which would normally be cut to a length of ¼ inch, and the fluffy grass surrounding the fringe, which would be cut to about 1 inch. You may have heard the expression, belly wedge. This is when you play the shot with your sand wedge, using a putting stroke, striking the ball on the centre line. Try it next time your ball finishes in such a position.

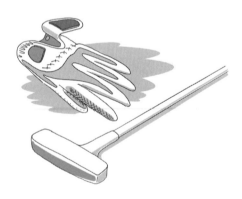

Breathe out to relax

Being uptight or tense when trying to hit a golf ball is fatal. Of course it happens more when you have a difficult shot to play or you are doing well in a competition. When you next address the ball on the practice ground, try inhaling and see how tense you become. Now try breathing out and see how relaxed you become. Breathe out, hit, then inhale. This needs practice just as much as you would practise a particular shot.

The costly slip!

Most of us use soft spikes on our shoes nowadays; they
have improved tremendously and of course they do not
damage the greens as much as the old metal spikes.
It is very easy to pick up wet grass cuttings or mud on
the soles so, on each tee, check that they are free from
anything that can make you slip.

Splash the ball onto the green from fluffy lies

An easy way to drop a shot is when your ball finishes within ten yards of the green in a fluffy lie. It's only just off the green but sitting down low in the grass. The two shots that are card wreckers are either catching the ball too high up, resulting in the ball shooting across the green, or quitting on the shot, resulting in the ball getting halfway. Play the shot out of the grass, the same way as you would play a bunker shot. Make sure you play it with a sand wedge and that the clubface is well open. Be positive and get that club under the ball. You will be surprised how often you are faced with this shot.

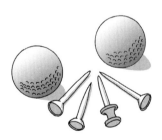

Shiny shoes

Do you know, I have never seen a great player with dirty shoes? To play your best you have got to feel and look the part. Can you imagine going for an interview for a very important job with mud on your shoes? Chances are, you would not perform to your best ability. If you get a great shine on your shoes you will look and feel good, remember that confidence is a big part of the game.

Keep your knees still

I am sure you have heard that you should keep your body
still when you are making your putting stroke. Easier said
than done! A foolproof and easy way is to keep your
knees still, which is much easier. Still knees, still body.

Practise chipping heights

Most of the time we tend to practise chipping with various clubs and rely on the loft of the club to control the height of the shot. This is all very well and can work to a certain degree but you can become better at those chip shots by varying the height the ball goes. First try hitting the ball a little lower by putting the ball back in your stance and shortening your follow through. You will notice the ball skids and then runs. Then try putting the ball a little forward in the stance which will make the ball fly higher. You will notice the ball comes down with very little backspin and very soon you will gain extra control.

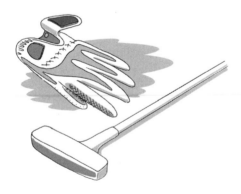

Be one step ahead

Nowadays, whether you are planning a golfing trip away from these shores or intend visiting a different part of the country to play some golf, it is important to book your golf in advance. My tip is to use the internet for your golf bookings. You can check out the type of courses, the cost for a green fee and surrounding attractions and facilities. Booking online gives you peace of mind and you can quite often benefit from discounted rates. Have fun planning your next golfing trip!

Your distance from the ball at address

In order to strike the ball consistently from the middle of the club face, it is important to stand the correct distance from the ball. Here is an easy way to remember: when you have set up to the ball with an iron, drop the club grip down onto your left leg, with the top of the grip four inches above your knee. When you are setting up to use a wood, drop the club grip onto your left leg with the top of the grip four inches above your knee.

That'll be inches, not feet, of course

Shots from old divots

Put yourself in the position where you have hit a super drive only to find the ball has come to rest in an old divot - you think you are the unlucky player in the tournament. The ball must be struck on the downswing, squeezing the ball out from the bad lie. 'Easier said than done', I can hear you saying. A great tip is to look at the front of the ball throughout the address and downswing; this will make you hit the ball first, then the turf. If it is a short iron you are playing, allow for plenty of backspin.

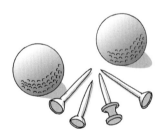

Reading the nap

In the U.K. we do not get very much nap on the greens; (nap is when the grass grows in one direction). In some countries the nap is stronger than the slope, which means that if the slope of the green is from right to left and the nap is from left to right, a putt will actually go up the hill. When you are playing an approach shot, if the green looks dark it means the nap is facing you, and the result will be for the ball to stop quickly. In this instance, try to pitch the ball up to the pin. When the green looks light and shiny the nap is growing away from you, which means the ball will land and roll, in which case you need to pitch the ball well short of the pin and allow for the roll.

45

An easy cure for that shank

The shank is a shot that can very easily make you give up the game, it can be like a disease you cannot get rid of. There are a number of reasons why a player shanks the ball, but they have one thing in common. By the time you have taken the club back and then returned it to the ball, the club head has got further away from you resulting in the ball being struck in the shank of the club. The cure is the opposite to what you would expect. I would like you to address the ball opposite the shank and try to hit the ball off the toe of the club. This will reverse your error and stop your shank immediately.

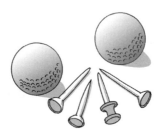

The worst weather I've ever had to play in

One year I was playing in the John Player Classic at Turnberry, Scotland and the forecast was terrible for the whole week. There was a pro/am the day before the tournament and the worst of the weather took place on that day. I finished my round, having been buffeted all over the place and went to the dry and warmth of the changing rooms. The first person I saw was a British comedian called Kenny Lynch, and I asked how he had got on. He told me he had been playing with Douglas Bader, a war hero who had lost both his legs. He was now walking and playing golf with the aid of artificial legs. Kenny went on to tell me that they had only played two holes when Douglas said, "Come on Kenny, got to go in, my legs are full". When he got inside they had taken off Douglas's legs and poured out the water. And we think we have troubles!

Look high to hit high, look low to hit low

Quite often it is not advisable to change your swing to deliberately hit the ball high or low. The best way is to address the ball and look high for the shot you want to fly high. You will notice that you will naturally put the ball a little forward in your stance, your weight will favour your back foot and you will picture a full follow through, all things necessary to hit the ball high. When trying to hit the ball low, look low. The ball will be addressed slightly back in your stance, your weight will favour your front foot and you will naturally shorten your follow through.

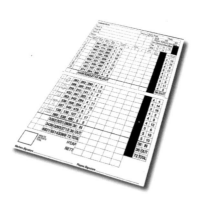

The bad first putt

If you were to hit your first putt within one foot of the hole every time, you would never three putt - well I certainly hope you wouldn't. Again pace is so very important.

Generally we do not practise long putting anywhere near enough and when we do, we put a bunch of balls down and putt them all to the same hole. When you are on the course you only get one go at a putt so practise that way. Put four or five balls on the putting green and putt one ball to five different holes. Do not be satisfied until each ball is within one foot of the hole. This type of practise will eliminate your three putts.

Take an energy drink out on the course with you

There are very few sports that take as long from start to finish as golf. Keeping your concentration and energy levels up during the second half of the round is difficult, therefore causing you to hit tiered shots and perhaps losing your match.

The Tour Professionals have realised that taking an energy drink as they start the back nine holes helps them maintain their energy and concentration levels. The most popular by far is a can of Red Bull. Do as the professionals do, you will be happy with the results.

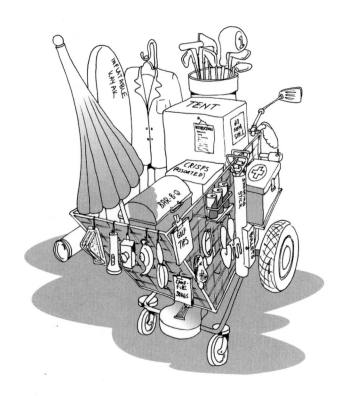

Be prepared for anything

The obvious things to remember are your clubs, your golf balls, your tees, your score card, a pencil, a pitch fork etc. The not so obvious things can also be very important, but easy to forget. Make sure you always keep a small first aid kit in your bag: things such as plasters in case of blisters, headache pills and insect repellent, can prevent you from having a miserable time out on the course.

Clean grooves for more control

One of the biggest differences between Tour Professionals and the weekend golfer is the way the professionals look after their clubs. They religiously keep the grooves on the iron faces clean and free from clogging. Many amateurs I teach allow the grooves on their irons to fill up with dirt so the ball is then unable to grip the face of the club. The result? No backspin.

Difficult shots made easy with the correct club

If your ball comes to rest just off the green in a lie, such as on a bare patch where players have walked to the next tee, or in an indentation where getting the club to the bottom of the ball is impossible, even a sandy lie that could easily cause you to duff the shot, then try putting the ball with a fairway metal. Strike the ball on the centre line and watch the ball run to the hole side. Difficult shots, made easy!

When those grips get wet

I do not believe that anyone likes playing golf in the rain, especially when it is pouring down and your grips get wet. We end up gripping so tightly that we cannot release the club head through the ball, resulting in loss of distance or even the club! At this point try gripping with a two-handed grip; this is when all fingers of both hands are gripping the club with no overlapping of fingers. It will help keep hold of the club and your right hand will more easily release the club through impact.

Rain-soaked glasses

If you wear glasses when you play golf you are at a definite
disadvantage when it starts to rain. The spots of rain get
onto the lenses and you can see a number of golf balls.
Wearing a cap or visor with a big peak is a help but wiping
the lenses with a cloth can smear them, making your vision
even worse. I have found that a small piece of chamois
leather wiped onto the lenses is great and can be used
very quickly and effectively.

That dreaded driving hole

Quite often there is a hole on the course that fills you with fear from the tee. Week after week it wrecks your card. Take five or six balls out to that tee one evening, when there is nobody about, and practise driving balls until you start hitting the ball onto the fairway. When you arrive there during your next round you will picture the ball landing on the fairway and the fear of that tee shot will be a distant memory.

Control the spin

I can almost hear you saying you would like to get some backspin, let alone control it! Club head speed and catching the ball before the ground will create plenty of back spin. If you want the ball to stop very quickly, maybe even to spin back, use a more lofted club; you will have to create lots of club head speed to get the distance required and the ball will stop dead. Sometimes you may not want the ball to stop so quickly, in which case, take a straighter faced club and hit the ball softer. The ball will land on the green and then release up towards the hole.

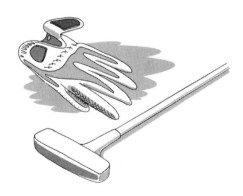

Keep your head warm

There cannot be many worse feelings than being on a golf course, miles from the clubhouse, when it's bitterly cold. If your hands are cold you cannot grip the club properly, if your body is cold you cannot turn properly. Put on a woollen bobble hat, you will find that your body stays much warmer. Think how cold your house would be if there was no insulation in the roof, it works the same way.

Mark your ball

You may have seen the Tour Professionals mark their ball with a permanent marker, some put dots above or below the number, some will put their initials, some draw a smiley face, etc. You may wonder why they do that, when they would check that they were playing with a different number ball from their opponent. Here is the reason...

If, when reaching your ball, you found another ball of the same make with the same number lying nearby that had been hit by a player not in your match, both balls would be deemed lost if you were unable to identify your ball. A two stroke penalty!

The same could happen if your ball ended up in the rough near a similar ball that had been lost earlier, making it impossible for you to identify which ball is yours. Same penalty! Get into the habit of putting your mark on the ball, and save those unnecessary penalties.

I'd recognise mine anywhere!

Improve your rhythm with Ernie

Even if you have a technically correct golf swing, you will hit bad shots if your rhythm is not good. You can look at this another way, even if you do not have a technically correct golf swing, you will hit many fine shots if your rhythm is good. I would recommend that you do as the best players do, either count one during the backswing and two during the downswing and follow through, or say Ernie during the backswing and Els during the downswing and follow through. Don't say it out loud, otherwise people will wonder about you!

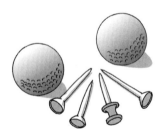

Are you getting caught up?

The ball has landed under a tree, wrecking any chance of
making a normal swing. It can result in an embarrassing
air shot or a thud as your club embeds itself into the top
of the ball. Set the club, look at the ball...and hit. If your
club keeps getting caught up in the branches at the top of
the backswing, then try setting your club at the top of the
backswing, well away from trouble. Leave the club where it
is, look down without moving your body and focus on the
ball. Now hit it. Just swing the club down and through the
ball.

Golf swing tips

Driving

How to drive the ball consistently

'Drive for show - putt for dough' is a famous saying. Well, if you do not drive the ball onto the fairway, you will not have many putts for dough. You will have plenty of putts to save, losing more dough. We seem to have a mental thing about needing to hit the ball harder with our driver than we do with any other club. A wild slash at the ball and so on.

The best tip I have heard relating to consistency with the driver is to try to make the best and most balanced swing you have ever made. This thought in your mind will encourage you to swing with more rhythm; it will also stop any kind of a slash at the ball. Try it this weekend, it will work.

How to drive the ball further

As a golf coach, the most common question I get asked is, how do I hit the ball further with my driver? Well, it is not by having a wild swipe at the ball as I explained in my previous tip. There are a few ingredients required, you can add one at a time and see the increased distance you hit the ball with your driver …

1.   Stand with your feet the width of your shoulders.
2.   Stand tall, this will help you create width in your swing.
3.   Make a complete 90 degree shoulder turn during your backswing. This is when your left shoulder points at the ball.
4.   At the top of your backswing, the knuckle on the thumb of your right hand should be well away from your right shoulder. This will create a wide arc.
5.   Start the downswing with an uncoiling motion from your left hip. At the same time keep the width in your arms (wide gap from the knuckle on your right thumb and your right shoulder). This will give you leverage.
6.   Do not be frightened to release the club head through impact. This creates club head speed.
7.   Turn right through onto your left foot; your belt buckle should now be facing the target.
8.   Hold onto a balanced follow through.
9.   Maintain your height throughout the swing.

You cannot possibly think of all these things in one swing, so perfect one move at a time and hit that ball further.

Hit the tee from under the ball

A great tip to keep you down through your drive swing is to try to hit the tee out from under the ball. If you are inclined to top the occasional drive, this will be the answer to your prayers.

Ball position

To hit the ball maximum distance when driving, the ball must be struck at the bottom of the arc or slightly on the upswing. It must not be struck during the downswing. The position of the ball at address will determine how the ball is struck. If the ball is too far back, you will strike it too early in your turn, making the ball go right. If the ball is too far forward, you will strike it too late in your turn, making the ball go left. I have always found the ball opposite the instep of my left foot is about right.

Cream
tee

Shaping the shot

Left to right

I bet there are a great number of you who can already shape the shot from left to right without trying, only trouble is, the ball does not end up where you want it to.

There are a few ways to make the ball move one way or another in the air, but the art is to land the ball on the spot you were aiming at. The best way to hit the ball with a controlled left to right spin is as follows:

1. Aim your feet, hips and shoulders in the direction you want the ball to start.
2. Open the club face until it points at the spot where you would like the ball to land. Then grip, do not grip before you open the club face.
3. Swing the club as you would normally, along the direction of your body. This will start the ball left of your obstacle.
4. Commit to striking the ball with the open club face.

The ball will come off the club with clock wise spin, turning the ball the required amount.

Right to left

To hit the ball from right to left take the opposite action to the previous tip.

1. Aim your feet, hips and shoulders in the direction you would like the ball to start.
2. Close the club face until it points at the spot you would like the ball to land, then grip. Do not grip before you close the club face.
3. Swing the club as you would normally, along the direction of your body. This will start the ball right of the obstacle.
4. Commit to striking the ball with a closed club face.

The ball will come off the club with anti-clock wise spin, turning the ball the required amount.

The punch shot

The punch shot can be very useful when you are playing on links courses, shots against the wind or even cross wind, when they are best kept low. The shot is normally played with either a medium iron or a short iron although there are players who use it with their longer clubs as well. When Tiger Woods plays his low drilling shot with a long iron or three wood, which he calls his stinger, it is played the same way as a punch shot.

When playing the punch, hold low down the grip, put the ball back in your stance, swing the club back to a position half way between your waist and shoulders, follow through just to waist height. The ball will go much lower, and with fizz.

Iron play

Long irons

I am sure that it is widely recognised that long irons are the hardest clubs to use. Do not fret, help has arrived in the form of a rescue club. It looks half iron, half wood and makes it easier to play shots of the distance for which you would normally use a long iron. I am sure it is the best introduction to the set of clubs for a very long time. If you have not got one, get one! The club is far more forgiving than the 3 or 4 irons, getting the ball into the air much quicker but still hitting the ball distances you would expect a good long iron to travel.

Long iron or fairway wood?

There is only one reason to use a long iron as opposed to a fairway wood, and that is when you are playing on a links course, trying to keep the ball low allowing it to run onto the green. Many links courses were designed for this type of shot and do not have bunkers guarding the front of the greens.

Sam Snead

Sam Snead played, tee to green, the best round of golf I ever saw. I had just finished my first round of the Benson & Hedges tournament at Fulford Golf Club in York. Sam Snead who was well into his sixties was just starting his round so I decided to go out and watch. Every shot he played had a slight fade from left to right. He hit every fairway and hit every green in regulation apart from three par fives which he hit in two. Amazingly, he too putted every green to score 69. If anyone else in the tournament had been putting for him, he would have broken 60.

At the end of the round a spectator asked him how he managed to get a long iron to stop so quickly on the green. Mr Snead asked how far the man hit his three iron, to which he replied that it was about 150 yards. Mr Snead's reply was "Why the hell do you want it to stop then!" I was surprised to see that after he had signed his card, he went straight to the practice ground to practise long shots; putting I would have understood but long shots, the way he had just played - wow!

I plucked up enough courage to ask why he was practising long shots after what was the best tee to green round I had ever seen and, as I said earlier, still is. He said that he had arrived at the course before his round and hit some warm up shots only to find that he was fading the ball; he decided to play the round with the fade and now he was on the practice ground trying to find out why he was fading the ball!

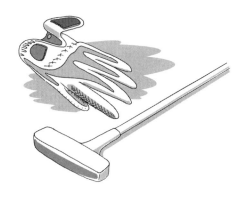

Mid irons

Know your distances

Accuracy is very important. We tend to forget that accuracy includes distance as well as direction, so it is important to know how far you hit each of your mid irons. The 5 iron through to the 7 iron are normally what we regard as mid irons. Of course it's not much help to know how far each club goes without knowing exactly how long a shot you have to play, so always have a yardage chart handy. To know how far you have to go and to know how far each club goes will give you loads of confidence to play the shot well.

The best players are always balanced when they play this shot, they never seem to be hurried and never try to hit the ball too hard.

Mid iron v. the wind

When playing a mid iron to the green always have one rule that you never break. If you are caught between two clubs into the wind, always hit the ball softer with the straighter faced club. Down wind, always hit harder with the more lofted club. If you do it the other way round, you will get too much elevation against the wind and you will quit on the shot down wind.

5 IRON :   YDS

GOOD DAY   150
BAD DAY   85
REALLY BAD DAY   40
ARGUED WITH WIFE 23½
PAY DAY   175
HANGOVER   6

Short irons

Technique

Always picture the ball fading in towards the hole, this will help you put the correct spin on the ball. Let me explain…

Stand in such a position that your feet, hips and shoulders are aiming just a little left of the target and position your feet a little closer together than you would for a mid iron; do this by moving your right foot closer to your left which will give the impression that the ball is back in your stance. Open the club face until it aims at the target. Now swing the club along a parallel line to your feet, striking the ball with the slightly open club face, giving it clockwise spin; this will move the ball slightly from left to right. For the low one, swing the club back to your waist height and through to waist height. For the high shot, always make a full follow through.

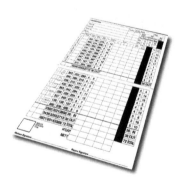

Soft arms

In a round of golf the short iron shot is used more than you may think. The best short iron players are the ones who create the most birdie opportunities. Feel is a very important factor with this shot, the best way for you to get this feel is to address the ball and relax your arms. We call this 'soft arms'. It will not be long before you are creating the birdie chances.

Take dead aim

You know it always amazes me when I watch a cricketer try to run one of the batsmen out, they pick up the ball, look at the wicket and throw, very often hitting the stumps. The reason they hit the stumps so regularly is because they are trying to. This sounds obvious, and it is to them. When you are playing your approach shot from say 100 yards, you should take dead aim and try to hole it. You will not hole all of them by any means, but you will set your sights higher and consistently get the ball closer to the hole.

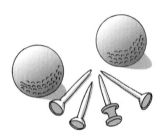

Get the ball up to the pin

If you were watching a competition from behind one of the greens you would notice that very few players ever get their approach shot up to the hole. Try aiming to hit the top of the flag when you are playing shots in with your short irons, this will encourage you to be a little bolder.

Fairway woods

Let the loft do the work

The best fairway wood players are the ones who hit the ball forward, letting the loft on the club get the ball in the air. This may sound obvious but most players go wrong by trying to help the ball in the air, resulting in hitting the ground before the ball or topping the shot. Commit to the shot and let the loft do its job.

The ball position

The fact that you are playing the shot with a wood does not mean that you address the ball as you would a driver. All clubs, apart from the driver, should be addressed with the ball 2 to 3 inches inside the left heel, when the ball is on the ground or teed up. All clubs have a graduation of loft from one to the next (normally 4 degrees), and if you start moving the ball backwards and forwards in your stance, you will affect that loft.

With the correct ball position, the ball will be struck during the downswing and the turf taken right after impact. This is necessary with all shots apart from a driver. The ball position for a driver should be opposite the instep of the left foot. This means, that with the same swing, you will hit the ball at the bottom of the arc or even slightly on the up swing, creating a more penetrating shot.

The only time to alter these ball positions is when you are deliberately trying to hit the ball high or low.

Addressing the ball

Chipping

You have a full set of putters in your bag!

If you are not comfortable playing a chip and run from just off the green, then putt the ball with one of your putters. In your golf bag all of your clubs are putters with varying degrees of loft. Simply choose the putter that has got the loft to carry the ball two to three feet onto the green with your normal putting technique, letting it run to the hole. This method has its advantages. When did you last duff a putt?

Chip too long?

If your chip goes past the hole, do not turn away in disgust. Keep watching the line the ball rolled past on, you will then have a much better idea of the line to take when putting the ball back into the hole.

Chip under an imaginary bar

Chipping the ball properly from off the side of the green can be very rewarding because it is a shot we are faced with time and time again. The ball should be struck in a way that makes the ball skid and then run towards the hole. The worst thing that can happen is for your left wrist to collapse through impact, resulting in a scooped shot.

1. First address the ball, holding at the bottom of the grip.

2. Position the ball towards the back foot.

3. Push your knees forward towards the target, this puts your weight onto the front foot and encourages a steep backswing and a steep approach into the ball (essential for this shot).

4. Imagine you are chipping under an imaginary bar, this will shorten your follow through to give the result you are looking for.

Pitching

Distance control

In order to get the best out of your game, it is vital to be able to control the distance you hit your pitch shots. If you hit your pitching wedge 100 yards with a full swing, what do you do when you only have 75 yards to go? If you try to hit the ball more softly, you will quit on the shot and mess it up. The distance control comes from the length of your backswing. If your full backswing pitching wedge goes 100 yards, then a three-quarter length backswing - shoulder height, will carry the ball 75 yards; a backswing to your waist height - half-way back, will carry the ball 50 yards. This technique is effective with all clubs.

Perfect one distance

It is extremely difficult to become very good from 70 yards, 80 yards, 90 yards and 100 yards so my best advice is to become brilliant from one distance. If at your practice range you have a target at say 90 yards, keep practising to that target until you are great at it. When you are on the course, try to leave yourself with an approach of 90 yards whenever possible. If your ball ends up 80 yards or 100 yards away, it is much easier to play a shot taking 10 yards off or adding 10 yards on to the length you are brilliant at.

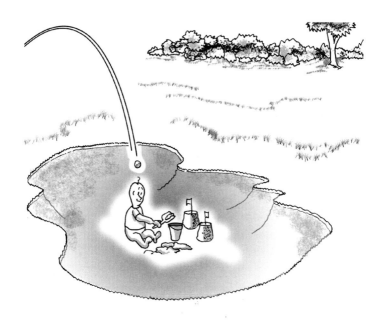

High pitch or low pitch?

The position of the pin will determine whether you should pitch the ball in low or high.

If the pin is at the back of the green, which would normally mean you have plenty of green to play with, a low pitch can be preferential. If the pin is at the front of the green or tucked in behind a bunker, then a high pitch would be better.

The low pitch

The low pitch is a very useful shot. It obviously flies in low but has plenty of backspin. Here's how to play the low pitch:

1. Position the ball back in your stance.

2. Grip the club at the bottom of the grip.

3. Put 60% of your weight on your left foot, 40% on your right.

4. Take the club back just to waist height.

5. Accelerate through, stopping your follow through at waist height.

6. Picture the ball flying in low.

The high pitch

Here's how to play the high pitch:

1. Position the ball towards your left foot (front foot).

2. Aim your feet, knees, hips and shoulders a little left of the target.

3. Aim the clubface at the target.

4. Swing the club along a parallel line to your feet (across the line of the shot).

5. At address, you will notice that the club head is in front of your hands. Make sure you swing the club, back, down and through, keeping the club head in front of your hands.

6. Picture the ball flying high and make a full follow through.

The lob shot

The lob shot has been around for many, many years. It was played by opening the face of a sand wedge, increasing the loft from 56 degrees to approximately 60 degrees. In actual fact many players still prefer to play it that way. The introduction of the Lob Wedge was fairly recent. This is a wedge that has 60 degrees of loft without opening the face of the club at all. For many players it has made the high flying pitch (lob shot) much easier to play. Whether you open the club face on a sand wedge or use a lob wedge, there are a couple of things you should know…

1. Cock your wrists quickly on the backswing.

2. Un-cock your wrists under the ball on the downswing.

3. Keep the club head in front of your hands throughout the swing.

4. Be positive!

The ball should land softly on the green with very little run. It is a good thought to try to slam dunk the ball, straight into the hole.

Bunker play

I have seen more players ruin their score by not being able to play from a bunker, than any other shot. There is a saying: A bunker shot is the easiest shot in the game. Not if you do not have a sound technique, in fact it can be a total nightmare. The fact that we are not allowed to touch the sand with our club before we play the shot stops us knowing the texture of the sand, or does it? When you next shuffle your feet into the sand to get a firm footing, take a mental note. You will be able to find out how soft the sand feels, how deep the sand is, if there are any stones or if there is any clay just beneath the surface of the sand. Knowing the conditions will help with the execution of the shot.

Back spin from the bunker

To get backspin from the green side bunker is fairly straightforward, it just needs practice. The size of circle you draw round the ball (refer to the greenside splash bunker shot tip) determines whether the ball will stop quickly or roll. To get backspin, draw a small circle of sand around the ball and splash that small circle onto the green. When you execute this correctly, the ball will spin plenty.

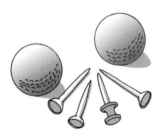

Getting roll from the bunker

Making the ball roll when it lands on the green from the bunker is again determined by the size of the circle you draw around the ball, and therefore the amount of sand you splash out of the bunker. Draw a larger circle round the ball, splash more sand and see that ball land on the green and roll.

Long bunker shot

If you have a long bunker shot, more often than not it is the result of having driven the ball into a fairway bunker. You will feel upset with yourself and then try to make up by trying to hit a miracle shot. Does that sound familiar? The first thing you must do is take a club that has enough loft to definitely get the ball out. There is no point in trying to get it out as far as possible using a straight faced club, only for the ball to hit the lip of the bunker and come back to where it started. Screw your feet well into the sand for a firm footing. Imagine the ball is sitting on a glass table top and all you have to do is hit it clean off the top, without breaking the glass.

Long Bunker
(for long bunker shots)

Bunker shot from the down slope

When playing a shot from the bunker down slope, it is natural to try to help the ball in the air; unfortunately that is the worst thing you can do. Stand parallel to the slope, then play the shot the same way as you would play from a flat lie. Feel you are splashing the ball down the slope and let the loft on the club get the elevation you need.

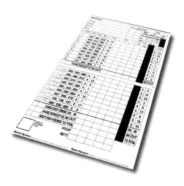

Bunker shot from the up slope

Normally this is an easier shot to play than the shot from a down slope, because you have the added loft of the slope to add to the loft on your club. Remember to hit this shot firmer because the ball will fly higher. Stand parallel to the slope and splash the ball out in the same way as you would from a flat lie.

The pot bunker shot

You will find pot bunkers on links courses (seaside courses). These bunkers tend to be very deep and relatively small in diameter. The only way out is with your most lofted club - a sand wedge or lob wedge.

1. Imagine the circle around the ball as mentioned in the splash shot.

2. Stand with your feet, hips and shoulders pointing left of the target (about 11 o'clock on a clock face).

3. Open the club face until it points at the target.

4. Swing the club along a parallel line to your feet (across the ball).

5. Cock your wrists very quickly on the backswing.

6. The secret is to increase the loft of the club under the ball.

The greenside splash bunker shot

Confidence probably plays a bigger part in the splash bunker shot than any other shot in the game. Believe it or not, it is the ball that puts us off. We are worried that, with the speed we have to hit the sand the ball will fly miles over the green if we catch the ball first, instead of the sand, so we take too much sand or quit on the shot altogether.

Next time you practise your bunker shots, leave the balls outside the bunker. Draw small circles in the sand, about 5 inches across. Now practise splashing those circles of sand onto the green. It is so easy because the ball is not there. Now go and get the balls, pop them into the bunker and draw a similar circle around the ball. Splash that same circle of sand onto the green, the ball will ride out on the sand and land where the sand lands. If you try not to make contact with the ball at all, only the circle of sand, this will help your confidence to such an extent that you will be telling everyone that bunker shots are the easiest shots in the game! Remember, you are not allowed to draw circles or even touch the sand when you are playing the course, it can only be done during practice.

A plugged lie in the bunker

We have all had them and I am sure we have all played them badly at some time. One great tip is to always let your opponent see the plugged ball before you play it, then you will have a valid excuse if the ball does not come out! Like all bunker shots, the club head has to get down below the ball to have any chance of coming out. The hard thing about playing the plugged shot is that you have to ensure your club goes lower through the sand than normal. There are two ways of playing the plugged shot, the method you choose is determined by the height of the bunker lip.

If the lip is low and you have plenty of green to play with, stand parallel to the line of the shot, square the club face, then drive the club down and through the sand. The ball will always roll quite a lot from this sort of lie. Experiment with both your sand wedge and your pitching wedge to see which one works best for you.

If the lip of the bunker is high, then use your sand wedge or your lob wedge, open the clubface wide, take the club back very steeply and then with all your strength bury the club under the ball. The ball should pop out.

Choosing a sand wedge

There are so many different shapes and styles of sand wedge it can be very confusing.
There are three main things to look out for:

1. The loft should be 56 degrees for a standard sand wedge and 60 degrees for a standard lob wedge.

2. Choose one that has a fairly rounded face, which will help when you want to open the club face, as you will not be put off by a sharp heel getting in the way and becoming too prominent.

3. Ensure your new club has plenty of bounce on the sole to help the club splash through the sand. You can do this by resting the club on the ground and looking to see if the leading edge is off the ground by approximately $1/8$ inch.

Egg sand wedge

My great friend, Gary Player

I wanted to bring my friend, Gary Player into my book and
I cannot think of a better place to introduce him than at
the end of the bunker section, Gary being the best bunker
player who ever lived.

I met Gary shortly after I had won the English Amateur
Championship at the ripe old age of nineteen. I had
just turned professional and was about to play my first
professional tournament, the Nigerian Open. He said to me
that if I played well in Nigeria and won enough money to
get to the South African Circuit, I could stay with him and
his family.

I was nineteen and Gary was World Number One;
opportunities like that do not come along very often. I
won the Nigerian Open and went to stay with Gary for four
months. I did the same thing for the next seven years. I
would like to say I won the Nigerian Open each year but
I did not. Apart from my parents and my wife Karen, Gary
has been the biggest influence in my golfing career.

I remember him getting letters from the best hotels in
South Africa, offering him the best suites, free of charge,
during the tournaments being played in their areas.
They just wanted to be able to say that Gary Player was
staying at their hotel. I used to travel with Gary to these
South African tournaments. He would check into the hotel
while I waited outside. About five minutes later a window
would open and Gary would shout down the number of his
room. That was my cue to pick up my luggage and move
in! He would order enough food for two on room service,

so I used to stay in the best rooms and eat for free at the best hotels in South Africa. It was his idea, I might add, not mine!

Gary had a beautiful house just outside Johannesburg in a place called Honey Dew. In the garden was a big putting green with a variety of bunkers surrounding it. Between 6am and 8am every morning we would practise bunker shots, he always insisted we played for something, normally five cents for the closest and one rand if either holed the shot. It used to cost me more than my air fare to South Africa each year! He once said to me that his sand wedge was his favourite club and that if he had to choose between it and his wife, he would probably miss her! All very tongue in cheek, of course. My friend is definitely one of the best players who ever played this wonderful game of golf.

Putting

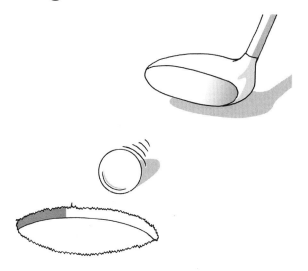

Let the putter head release

If you are struggling with your putting it can often be because you have allowed your stroke to become too mechanical. For a period of time the accepted way to putt was with a rocking motion from the shoulders, keeping the wrists firm. This can work for some but not for all. Try letting the putter head release slightly through impact, this will give you more feel, which I believe is essential in achieving consistent pace.

Move your chin to alter your backstroke

If you like to stand well away from the ball when you set up for your putt, i.e. a line from your eye to the ground would be between your feet and the ball, then your putter should travel on a slight arc (in - square - in). If your eye is above the line the ball is on, then the putter should travel straight back and straight through. If you find your putter is going back outside the line you would like, try moving your chin a little to the right so you are looking more through your left eye, this will encourage the putter to come a little more inside on the way back. Try doing the exact opposite if your putter comes too far inside during the backswing.

Bread & putter

Three ways to stop the yips

Players who have not experienced the yips should count themselves lucky, believe me. Having the yips is no joke. It is when your right hand decides to have a mind of its own during the impact of a putt, your mind says one thing but your right hand takes no notice.
Most sports that require either hitting or throwing have players who will suffer this feeling. The key is to take the normal hinging of the right hand out of the stroke by using one of the following tips:

1. Grip the putter left hand below the right and much firmer with your left than your right. Feel as though the left hand and arm are totally in control and that your right hand is just going along for the ride.

2. Use the claw grip. This is when your right hand grips the putter in between the middle finger and the index finger. This will encourage a pushing motion from the right hand rather than a releasing of the club head motion.

3. Putt left handed. Players on both the European Tour and the PGA Tour have been very successful in doing this.

Keep putting stats

It is amazing how often we blame our putting when we have a bad score. We remember the putts we missed and forget the ones we holed. Always count and write down how many putts you had in your round - only putts from on the green. Do this over a period of 10 rounds and see what your average is. If it is below 30 that is very good, so you can stop blaming your putting for bad scores. If it is above 33 then practice is needed. Anyone can be a good putter, it does not need strength, just practice.

Get a putter with loft

There are so many putters to choose from these days that it can be very confusing. It is important you choose carefully, because they are mostly expensive and you will use your putter for more shots than any other club. Always choose a putter that has a little bit of loft because when you strike the ball, your hands will be slightly in front, which de-lofts the club. Putters with no loft therefore have minus loft through impact and the ball bounces as soon as the ball is struck.

Taking too long over your putts?

Remaining relaxed when you are putting is very important, I am sure you will agree.
Standing over the putt for too long will make you more tense, so I would suggest you decide on the line, address the ball, look at the hole twice and then putt. The more times you look at the hole the more negative thoughts you will have.

Sloping green

When you have a putt that is going to move from right to left or left to right, look at the part of the hole where the ball will enter. If you expect the ball to go into the front of the hole on sloping putts, the chances are, you will miss the putt on the low side.

Accelerate the putter

Whether you are faced with a long or short putt, you must accelerate the putter through the ball. The best way to achieve this is to shorten your backswing a little, which will encourage you to accelerate through.

Hit those six foot putts a little firmer

It is quite possible to be tentative on the short putts and lose all confidence. Try this great tip: practise by putting a ball two inches in front of the hole, and then from six feet putt your ball hard enough to knock the other ball into the hole. This will train you to be positive and hit those short putts a little harder.

Green imagination

Getting the ball up to the hole on uphill putts and stopping the ball from going too far on downhill putts can be a problem. Next time you play golf, imagine a hole is cut about one foot past the real hole on uphill putts and about one foot short of the hole on downhill putts. Then try to hole the ball into the imaginary hole.

Hover the putter

Taking the putter away smoothly is a big help. If you find this difficult, try hovering the putter about 1/8 inch above the putting surface, you will find the putter will go back at about half the pace.

Use the rules to your advantage

Knowing the rules can help you; here are a few that you need to know:

Local rules

Knowing all or even most of the rules of golf is just about impossible and the key is to know where to look up the rule in the book. Local rules are always on the back of the score card and the notice board at the golf club; make sure you read these rules because they over-rule the rules of golf. A great example is stones in bunkers. In the rule book you will notice that you are not allowed to remove stones in bunkers but, quite often, the local rule for the course allows the removal of stones in bunkers. So, if a stone is impeding your shot, it pays to know the rule!

When is the ball in a hazard?

A hazard will be marked by a red or yellow line, depending whether it is a water hazard or a lateral water hazard. Your golf ball is deemed to be in the hazard when the ball touches a part of the line, unlike an out-of-bounds white line where the entire ball has to be over the line.

Casual water

Did you know that your ball is regarded as being in casual water when it is lying in surface water on or off the fairway? It is also in casual water when you are able to squelch up water, whilst taking your stance. The rule says that you can drop the ball within one club length from the closest point of relief. This means that if your ball is in casual water in the rough and the closest point of relief is on the fairway, you are allowed to drop on the fairway.

Out of bounds

For your ball to be out of bounds and to incur a two-shot penalty, the entire ball has to be over the out of bounds margin.

Drop the ball correctly

During your round you may have to drop your ball, either as a free drop or under penalty. This is how you drop correctly:

If you are entitled to a free drop you will be able to drop the ball within one club length of the closest point of relief. You can use any club to measure that one club length, it does not have to be the club you intend playing the shot with. Measure the distance by laying the club down on the ground and then putting a tee in the ground at the one club length distance. Now stand facing the target, from waist height and from an outstretched arm to the side of your body, drop the ball within the club length. If the ball happens to roll outside the club length, that is fine, providing it does not come to rest either nearer the hole or more than another two club lengths outside the tee that you put down as measurement, in which case you have to drop again. If your drop is under penalty and the rule says you have to drop within two club lengths, exactly the same procedure applies, except that the measurement is two club lengths instead of one.

Rabbit scrape under a bush

This can be an awkward one. If your ball is in a rabbit scrape under a bush, it may not give you the free drop you were expecting. You only get a free drop if you can see a way of playing the shot, though not if it is impossible to hit the ball - in this case you would have to drop the ball under a penalty of one shot. If your opponent asks for a free drop from a rabbit scrape under a bush, ask whether they would have tried to play the shot from there, if the ball was not in the scrape. If they say no, do not give them a free drop.